CLASSICAL GUITAR SOLOS
for All Occasions

ARRANGED BY JERRY WILLARD

ISBN 978-1-5400-3415-1

HAL•LEONARD®

Visit Hal Leonard Online at
www.halleonard.com

Contact Us:
Hal Leonard
7777 West Bluemound Road
Milwaukee, WI 53213
Email: info@halleonard.com

In Europe contact:
Hal Leonard Europe Limited
42 Wigmore Street
Marylebone, London, W1U 2RN
Email: info@halleonardeurope.com

In Australia contact:
Hal Leonard Australia Pty. Ltd.
4 Lentara Court
Cheltenham, Victoria, 3192 Australia
Email: info@halleonard.com.au

INTRODUCTION

Jerry Willard

Welcome to *Classical Guitar Solos for All Occasions*. The pieces in this folio have been culled and arranged as an aid to the working professional and semi-professional guitarist who finds himself in a variety of playing situations, such as weddings, restaurants, and other social gatherings that present live music. Amateur players will also benefit from this eclectic resource of selections—from timeless classics to sacred music—that would be appropriate for these types of events and settings. Students will find a wealth of non-traditional recital and audition pieces that will impress their colleagues and contemporaries.

Included are pieces from the Renaissance and Baroque periods that work very well for weddings, in addition to the famous wedding songs by Wagner and Mendelssohn. There are Christmas carols that can be performed as solo pieces or as duets with vocals, and traditional pieces from the standard repertoire that are ideal as background music.

The music is presented in standard notation and tablature, with page turns minimized for easy reading. This book is essential for classical guitarists, steel-string fingerpickers, and electric guitar players who wish to round out their repertoire with classical and fingerstyle music. I have included optional flute and voice parts for those pieces commonly played in this combination.

TABLE OF CONTENTS

Titles presented in level of difficulty. See page 112 for an alphabetical index.

Vaghe Belleze Et Bionde Treccie D'oro Vedi Che Per Ti Moro

Anonymous 16th century Italian

Bianco Fiore

Cesare Negri *(c.1535–c.1604)*

Se Io M'accorgo

Anonymous *16th century Italian*

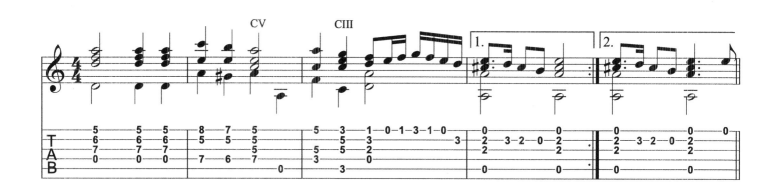

Danza

Anonymous *16th century Italian*

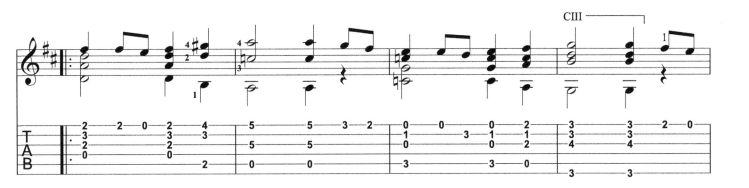

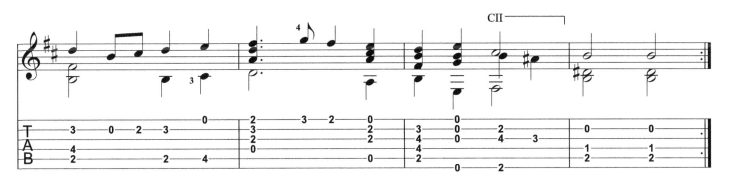

Saltarello

Vicente Galilei *(c.1520–1591)*

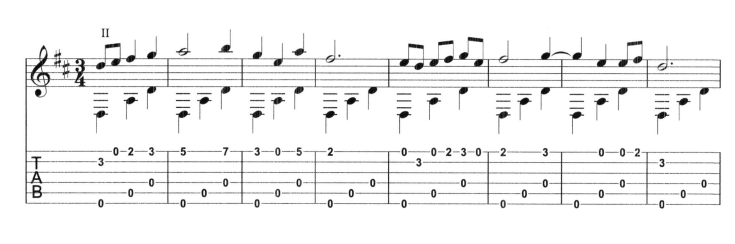

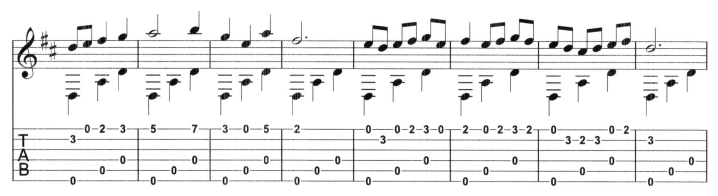

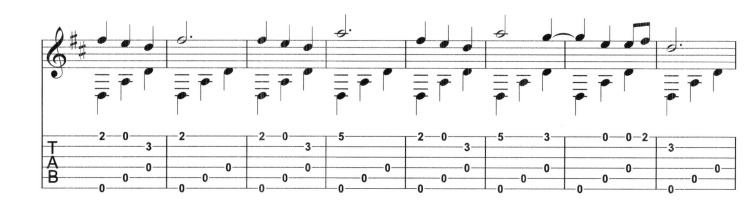

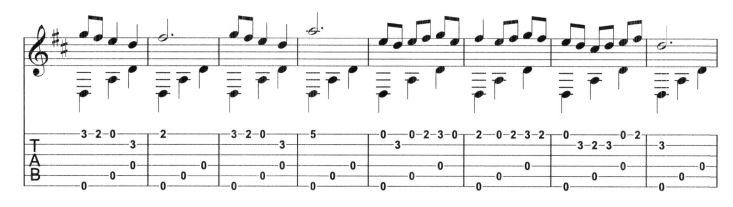

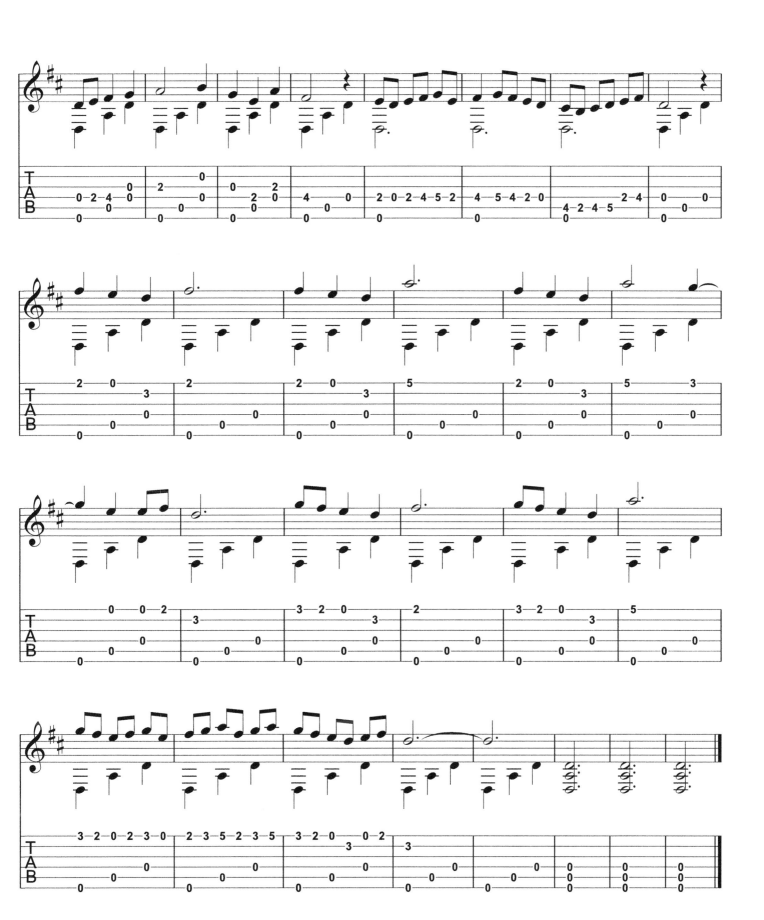

Pavana

Luis de Milán *(c.1500–c.1561)*

Guardame Las Vacas

Luis de Narváez *(1490–1547)*

Kemp's Jig

Anonymous *16th century English*

Mrs. Nichols' Almain

John Dowland *(1563–1626)*

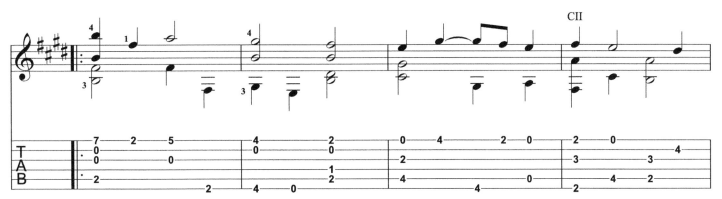

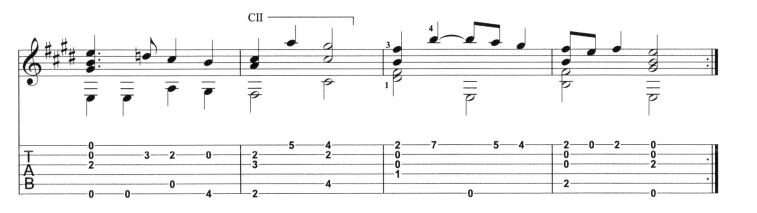

Greensleeves

Anonymous *16th century English*

Almain

Francis Cutting *(1550–1603)*

Moderately

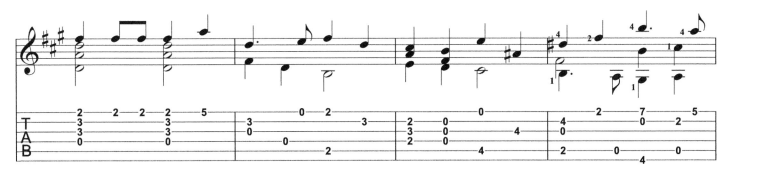

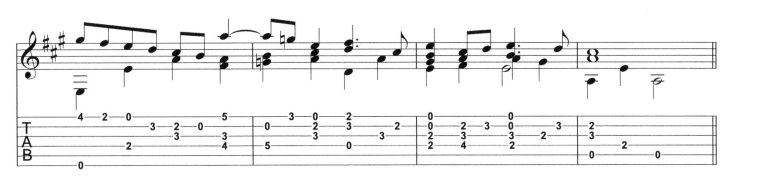

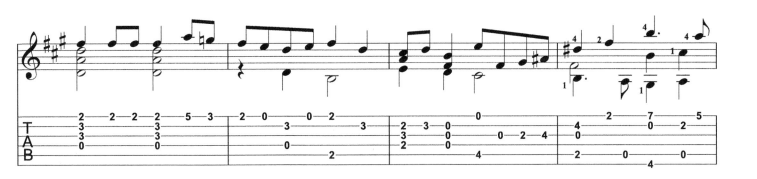

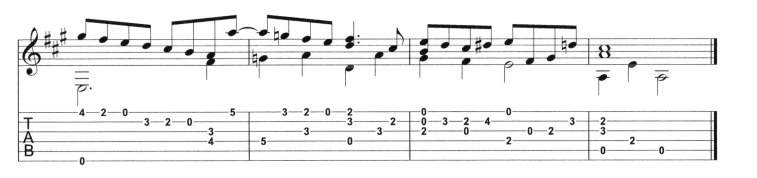

Lady Hunsdon's Puffe

John Dowland *(1563–1626)*

Moderately

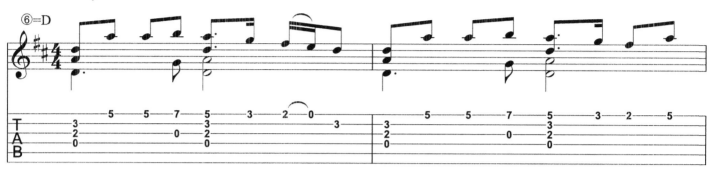

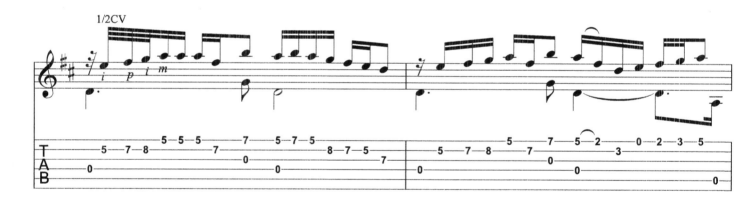

Pavanas

Gaspar Sanz *(1640–1710)*

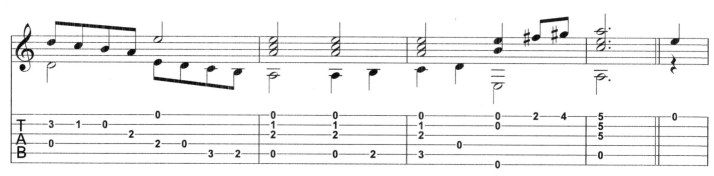

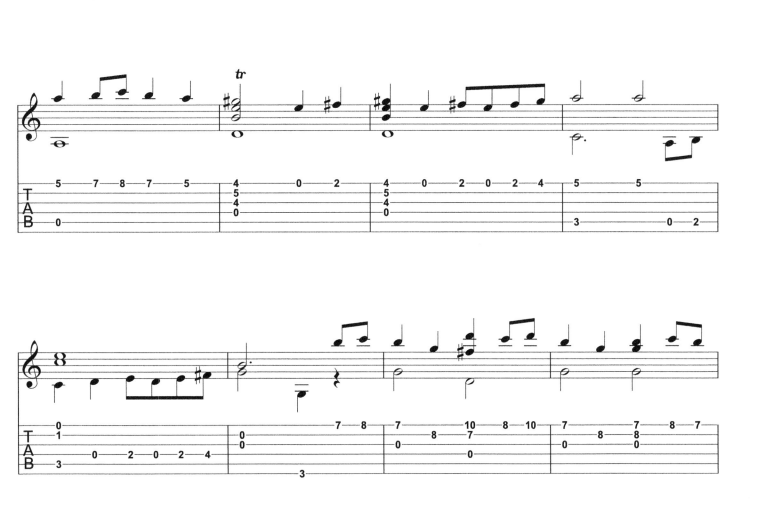

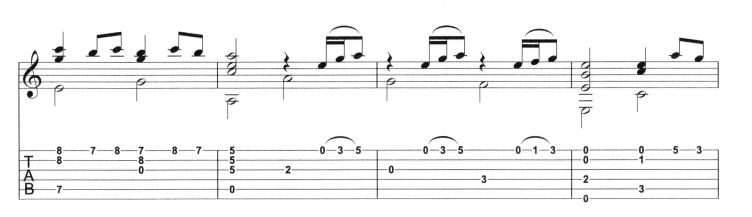

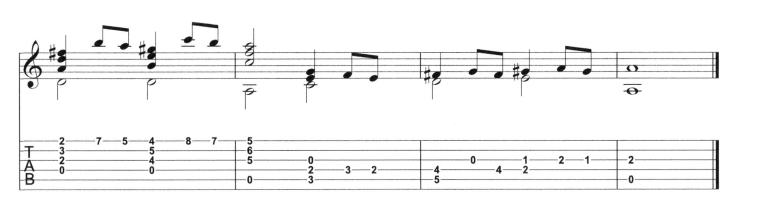

Almain

Robert Johnson *(1583–1633)*

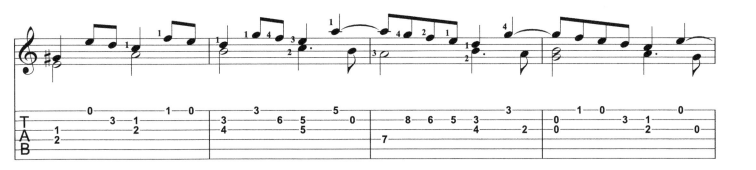

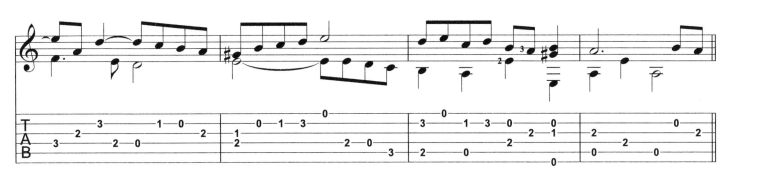

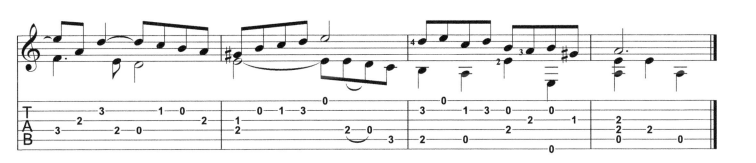

Gavotte

Johann Sebastian Bach *(1685–1750)*

Gavotte 1

Gavotte 2

D. C. Gavotte 1 al Fine

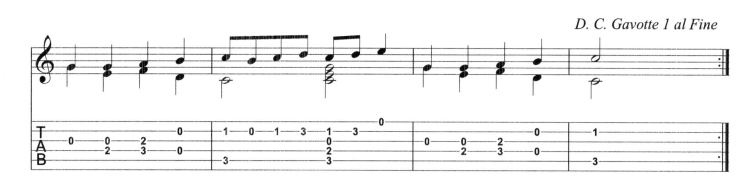

Canarios

Gaspar Sanz *(1640–1710)*

Passacaille

Robert de Visée *(1660–1725)*

Rondeau

Jean-Joseph Mouret *(1682–1738)*

Moderate march

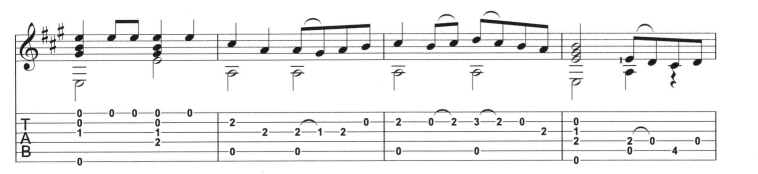

Minuet in G

Johann Sebastian Bach *(1685–1750)*

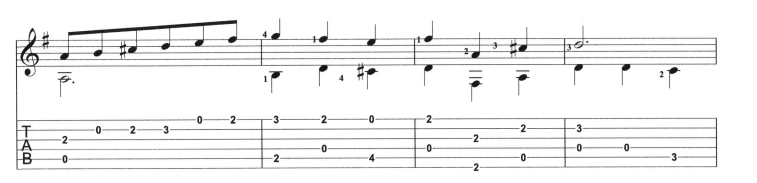

Bist Du Bei Meir

Johann Sebastian Bach *(1685–1750)*

Air on the G String

Johann Sebastian Bach *(1685–1750)*

Jesu, Joy of Man's Desiring

Johann Sebastian Bach *(1685–1750)*

Prelude

Johann Sebastian Bach *(1685–1750)*

Bourée

Johann Sebastian Bach *(1685–1750)*

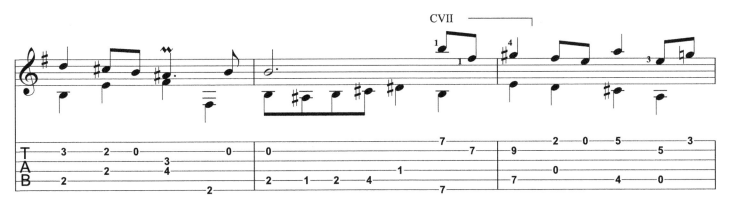

Sheep May Safely Graze (Theme)

Johann Sebastian Bach *(1685–1750)*

In Dulci Jubilo

Anonymous *16th century German*

Moderately

God Rest Ye Merry, Gentlemen

Traditional *English Carol*

Moderately

Away in a Manger

James R. Murray *(1841–1905)*

Slowly

Away in a Manger

W. J. Kirkpatrick (*1838–1921*)

A Virgin Most Pure

Traditional *English Carol*

Moderately

Doxology

Louis Bourgeois *(1510–1561)*

Hava Nagila

Traditional

Moderately

God Save the King

Henry Carey *(1687–1743)*

Pomp and Circumstance

Sir Edward Elgar (1857–1934)

Slowly

Plaisir d'amour

Jean Paul Martini *(1741–1816)*

Slowly

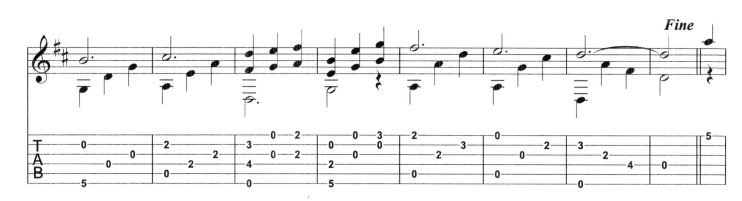

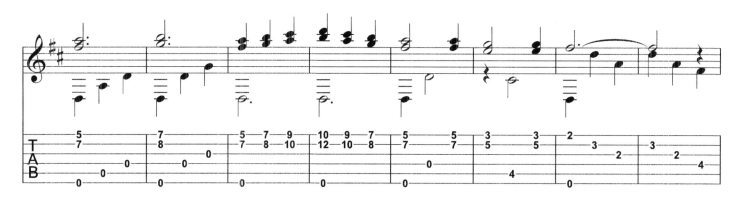

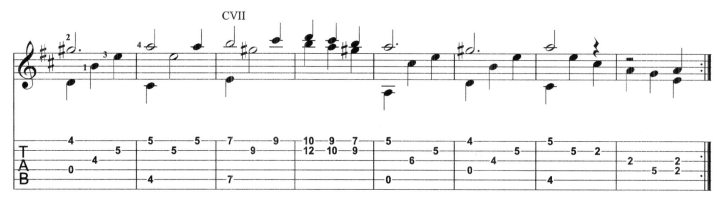

Bridal Chorus

Richard Wagner *(1813–1883)*

Moderately

Melody Instr. Optional

Wedding March

Felix Mendelssohn-Bartholdy *(1809–1847)*

Majestically

Melody Instr. Optional

March from *The Magic Flute*

Wolfgang Amadeus Mozart *(1756–1791)*

Slowly

Ode to Joy

Ludwig van Beethoven *(1770–1827)*

Estudio

Francisco Tárrega *(1852–1909)*

Study No. 5

Fernando Sor *(1778–1839)*

Study No. 3

Matteo Carcassi *(1792–1853)*

Andantino

Study No. 7

Matteo Carcassi *(1792–1853)*

Les Folies d'Espagne

Mauro Giuliani *(1781–1829)*

Andantino

Variation 2

Variation 3

Variation 4

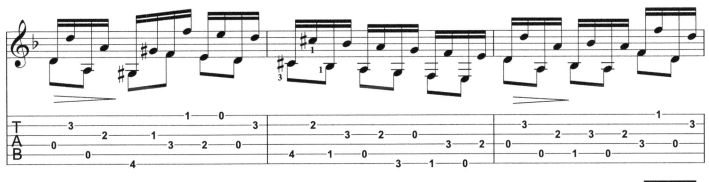

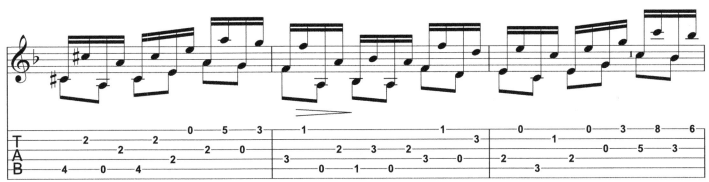

Variation 5

Variation 6

Allegro vivace

Romance

Anonymous

Slowly

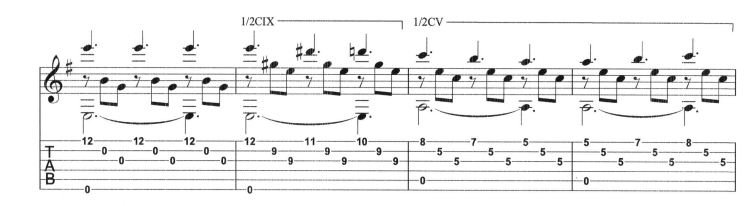

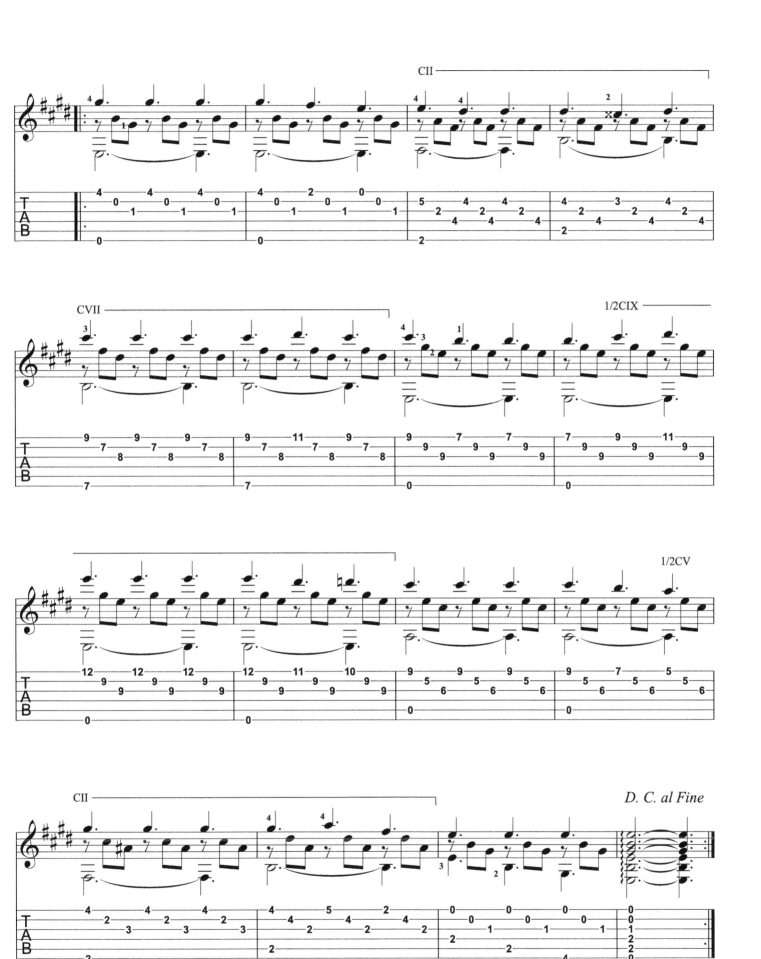

Lágrima

Francisco Tárrega *(1852–1909)*

Adelita

Francisco Tárrega *(1852–1909)*

Gymnopédie No. 1

Erik Satie *(1886–1925)*

Lent et douloureux

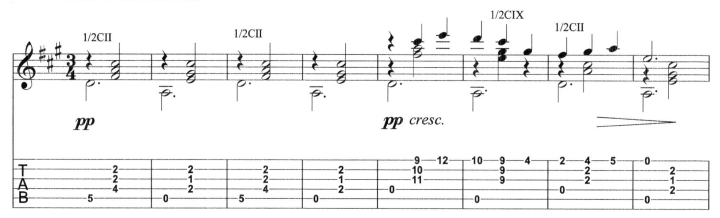

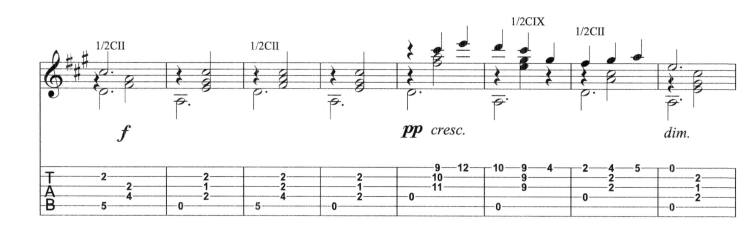

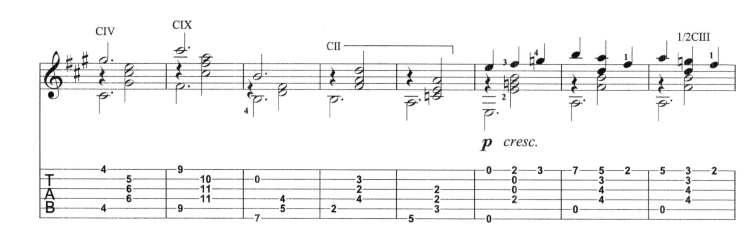

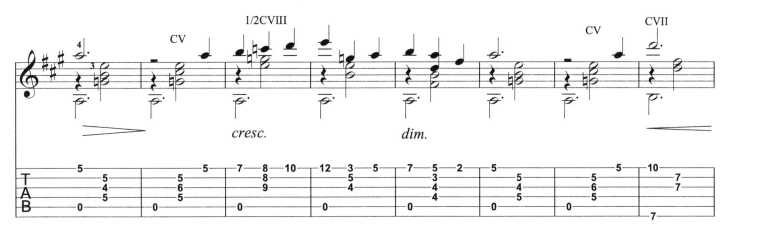

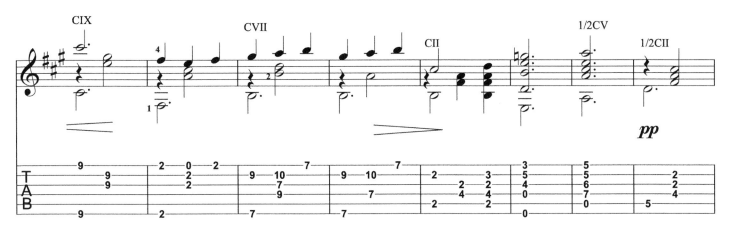

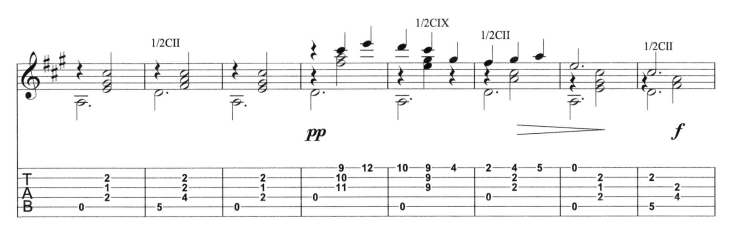

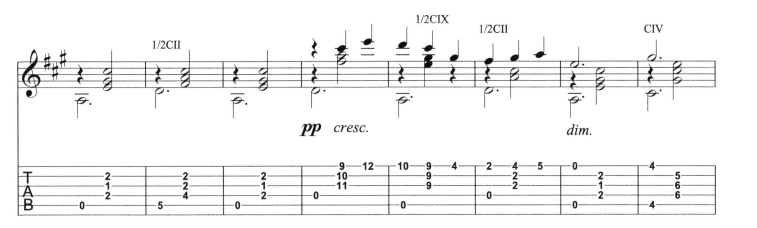

Capriccio Arabe

Francisco Tárrega *(1852–1909)*

Recuerdos de Alhambra

Francisco Tárrega *(1852–1909)*

Andante

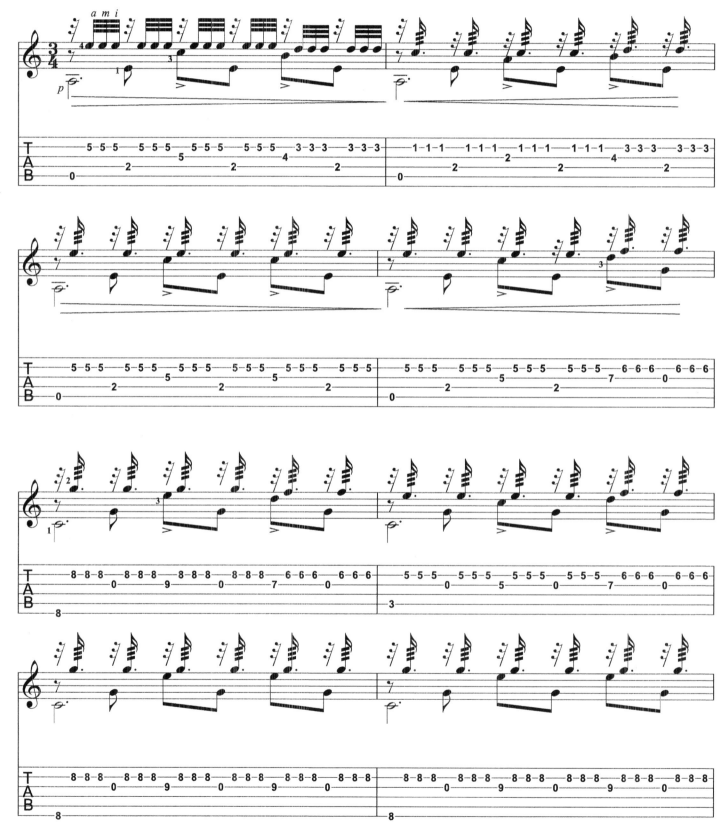

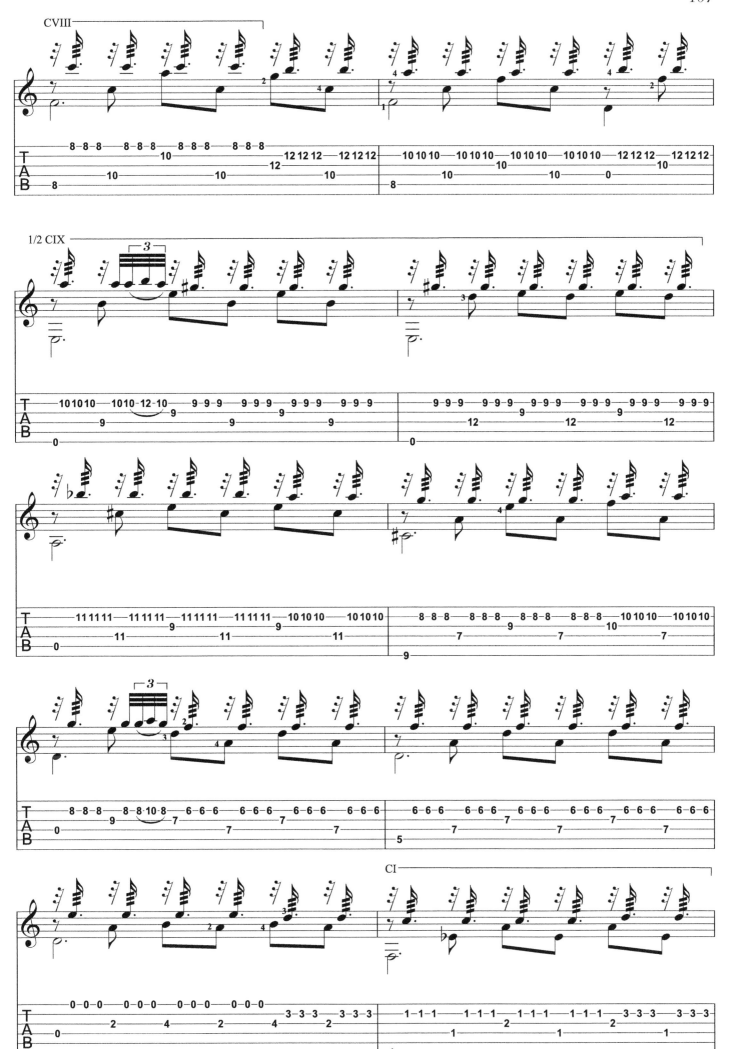

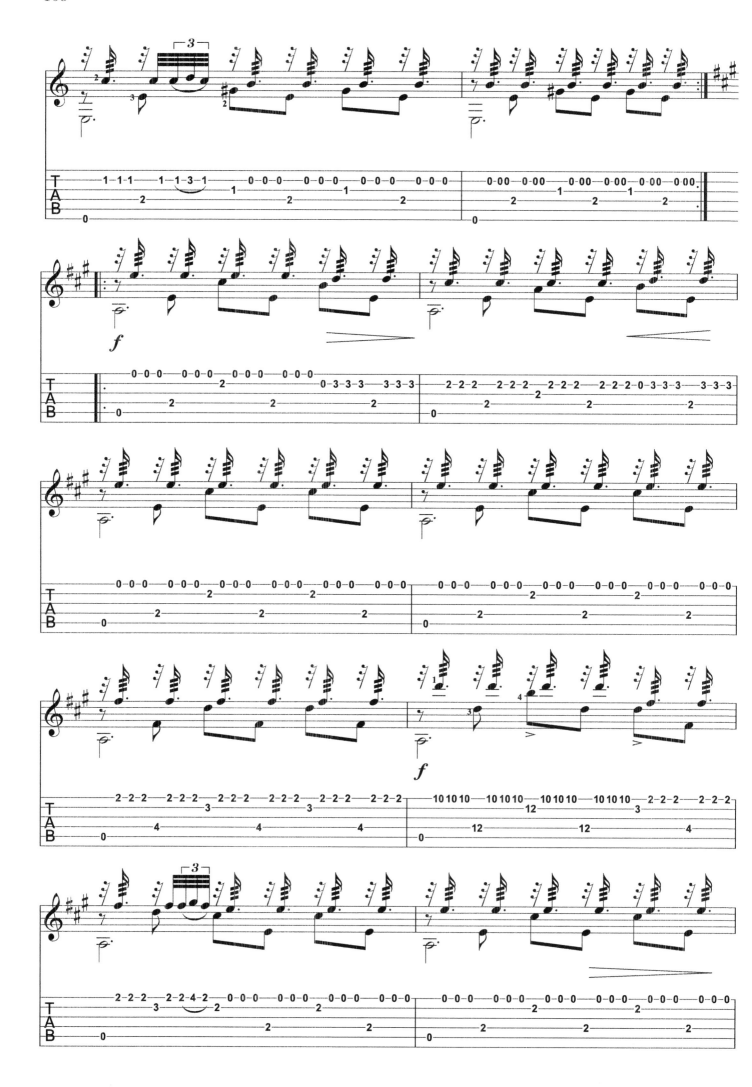

Coda

INDEX

Alphabetical by Title